Sunlit Reflections

Tina Singh

BookLeaf Publishing

India | USA | UK

Made with ❤ on the BookLeaf Publishing Platform
www.bookleafpub.in
www.bookleafpub.com

Dedication

To my sister, Dolly, whose encouragement inspired me to share my words with the world.

Preface

In the quiet corners of my life, I discovered poetry as a way to channel my thoughts, dreams, desires, and emotions. What began as a personal journal, adorned with the artistic flair of imaginative reflection, evolved into a deeply meaningful practice. I found inspiration in the everyday—sometimes a phrase, a word, or a fleeting moment would ignite a poem. Other times, I penned verses for my future self, capturing hopes, dreams and challenges yet to unfold.

For many years, my poetry remained a private endeavor, a collection of musings I never imagined sharing publicly. But when the opportunity arose to publish my work, I felt a gentle nudge - a call to invite others in. My older sister, Dolly, who read my early scribbles and encouraged me to publish, often echoed in my thoughts.

These pages hold my thoughts and reflections—imperfect yet authentic. They are my way of reaching out, of holding out my hand to connect with the rest of humanity. If my words can resonate, offer solace, or simply remind you that you are not alone, then I welcome you to join me on this journey.

Acknowledgements

I am incredibly grateful to BookLeaf Publishing for providing this opportunity for amateur writers like myself to share our voices and stories. Thank you for empowering and believing in us.

To my sister, Dolly, thank you for always being there to read my drafts and for encouraging me to take the leap into publishing.

To my dear friend, Hussam, our exchanges of poems have not only inspired me but also strengthened our bond. Thank you for being a constant source of motivation.

A heartfelt thank you to my aunt, Mohinder Kaur. You taught me about the true power of words, which has shaped my understanding of poetry and its impact.

To my friends and family, many of whom have inspired my works in countless ways, your presence in my life has been a vital part of my creative process.

This collection is a reflection of all your influences, and I am grateful to share it with you.

Hold My Hand

Imprint to imprint
Mountains collide
As valleys converge

Gentle yet firm
You hold the tangible portal to my soul
In your very own.

Character, strength and courage
The eternal wisdom of lessons learned
Lie in each callous, wrinkle and treasured imperfection.

Subtle is the residual fragrance
A memory of the intimate spark
Created upon that first union.

Interlocking
We joined our lines of destiny
In the perfect embrace.

Apologies

"I'm sorry," I said. My words hung in the air – a manifestation of my vulnerability for all to see. Propelled into the sky as if emitted from a megaphone, laced with the frills of my deepest sincerity, they remained suspended.

Frozen.

Paralyzed.

Like a trapeze artist who has released herself mid-air without a swing to rescue her, my words plummeted to their demise in your silence.

If an apology is delivered and there is no one to acknowledge its receipt, what becomes of those words? They wander aimlessly in the purgatory between rejection and acceptance, questioning the meaning of their lives.

I uttered this orphaned phrase and waited…anticipating the response for a brief but intense moment before I felt something change inside me forever. These words marked the conception of a sentiment that led to a pregnant pause which has lasted 3 months.

In other words: an eternity.

You never accepted my apologies. Never even acknowledged this private and sensitive exposure of my flaws that I selectively chose to share with you. And by doing so, I let you diminish my worth in your eyes.

The silence that enshrined my thoughts and emotions when I was too weak to speak my mind for fear that they would suffer the same fate as my apologies….

has finally come to an end.

As I bend to sweep up the remnants of a disintegrated apology whose stale ashes lie at the ground in front of your feet, I stand renewed and determined.

With the death of my confession comes a rebirth.

To the woman I was before I met a man who rendered me speechless for all the wrong reasons.

To the girl I was before love and the fear of heartbreak
placed a muzzle on my spirit.

I am human and will admit my faults. But never again
will I allow another to determine my worth

as a woman
a companion
a lover
as a friend.

Accept me, reject me, judge me if you must.

Sorry. I'm not sorry.

Flashback

Eyes open. Staring
Heart open. Reminiscing

Burning...stinging...intensifying
A faint memory
Unearthing deep sentiment

Tears flowing. Inside and out.
A physical manifestation
Of an emotional memory

Recollections long forgotten
Repressed...buried
With his love

Wretched realization
Raw remorse
Escalating...

Blink.

Lesson Learned

The hunter and the hunted. Tired of running, we stood face to face; neither of us quite understanding how we both became collateral damage in a war that was not our own.

For a brief moment in time, there was a stillness in the air. A silence that eliminated the chaos, followed by the sweet melody of your voice. A sense of clarity and purpose dissipated the fog that had come to reside in my mind.

I loved you on purpose. Because of my heart and notwithstanding my better judgment. In spite of your faults, your imperfections and your determination for danger, I invited you to touch my soul.

That space I created for you was Sacred. Personal. Unique. It was a place of hope and carefree timelessness that you inspired within me.

I gave to you my vulnerability with a clear message:
Handle With Care. And I believed your sincerity when
you gave me your promise.

There was honesty in your lies, and deception in your
truth. Your actions spoke louder than your words, but
your feelings betrayed your every move. I saw the
reluctance in your eyes and sensed the hesitation of your
touch well before we reached our final destination.

We played a risky game of calculated emotional
reciprocity that ended in failure. And for this, I blame
you. It takes two to tango but one to commit the fatal
misstep that stops the music.

As the sound of your voice fades, I embrace the familiar
fog with a new sense of resolve. You entered my life for a
reason, stayed for but one season; but what you gave me
will last a lifetime.

No regrets.

Hate That I Love You

You walked into my life. You opened my eyes. And you stole my heart.

I hate you.

You targeted my soul, captured my spirit and held it hostage to your perfect love.

You let me fall into your arms; an instant and warm surrender that made logic and reason irrelevant – and emotion, desire and passion the only reality worth embracing.

Because of you, I gained entry into the fantasy that only the pure and innocent know. The fantasy I secretly prayed for but was never bold enough to request.

You offered this to me on a silver platter; never asking for anything in return, though I unabashedly gave you myself willingly and without hesitation.

Forcibly, your love invaded my heart; breaking down the
brick walls of fear and mistrust that had faithfully
guarded it since birth.

Subtly, your spirit joined forces with my own,
intertwining its essence into the fibers of my being, until
I could no longer separate strands foreign from native.

Gently, you filled my life with a hope that had no
hope. Inadvertent deception was the song you played as
we danced, brashly denying the ephemeral nature of our
existence.

When the music stops, the curtain descends. Stage lights
give way to the darkness and we are but two lonely
silhouettes in an empty room...wishing.

Eyes open. Heart stolen.

I love you.

Pardon Me

Pardon me for asking your name twice
My heart skipped a beat the first time and I couldn't
concentrate.

Pardon me for stuttering when I speak to you
I can't seem to control my lips when you're near me.

Pardon me for requesting your presence in my dreams
You make the experience that much better.

Pardon me for relying on your strength and
encouragement
Sometimes it's the only thing that keeps me sane.

Pardon me for wanting your last name,
Only so I may place it properly behind my own first.

Pardon me for loving you with all my heart,
You give me no choice.

Angel of Death

I lied to you.

With every ounce of my being I insisted, pleaded, convinced you that my lie was the truth; that your faith was well placed in my human hands.

You trusted me. You shared with me your deepest, darkest fears. In exchange for your trust, I gave you what I wanted for you: a lie.

I let my unchecked and unfounded confidence take the lead, leaving only my empathy and compassion to play supporting roles in our saga.

I sit here now with a lump in my throat, an ache in my stomach and tears in my eyes. I unknowingly abused a power I should never have had, barely noticing the ramifications of my words.

My knees are too weak to carry my heavy heart as I kneel outside your room. A symbol of health and hope, my white coat now offers only an agonizing reminder of what could have been.

I was the last person you trusted. She who vowed to first do no harm ironically dealt you an unforgiveable disservice in your final moments. And for this – I repent.

That is the truth.

MD

Imagine...
Raw, unadultered stench
Permeating every crevice
Of your physical being.

Picture...
Rotting, limp flesh
Clutching bone
Tenaciously praying for life.

Listen...
To the final breath
Uncontested
Save by a single tear.

Experience...
Mourning your own soul
existing only in memory.
The future holds no meaning.

Bear...
The burden of his words
The echo of fate
"Estas muriendo."

A Beautiful Soul

A soul ensheathed in a fragile sleeve
The body

Longing to breathe but finding no air
Suffocating

Searching for a way to satiate a thirst
Slowly withering

Birth marks the beginning of this battle
A lifelong struggle

A battle wrought over a caged spirit
Taking journey for decades on Earth

Search in life for an elusive essence
Embraced only in Heaven after death.

Today commemorates an emancipation

A freedom so profound
A celebration of life
And a testament of worth

...for a beautiful soul

Rest in Peace.

Dream

The stage is set.
The curtains open.
The show begins.

Your life:
A screenplay in real time
Authored by your hopes

You are the narrator
The protagonist
And the audience

Your vision is blurry
But the message is clear:
Prepare for the future.

You watch yourself
Experiencing anticipation,
Uncertainty, and then elation

An overwhelming joy
Paralyzing in its perfection
An answer to your prayers

Unbelievably gratifying
And too good to be true
Literally.

It was only a dream.

Misplaced

I didn't have to try.

I stumbled upon you unwittingly. I kept you. I cherished you. But I also took you for granted.

You left. Without a word. Without a real goodbye. As though you were never mine to begin with.

Instead of mourning your loss. Instead of searching for you. I recreated you in my mind.

Constructed a mirage so perfectly deceptive that I convinced myself that you were here.

That I still had you, wrapped in my arms. That you would never leave me...as long as I believed.

The false promises I told myself cheated me out of reality; a reality that I needed to bring you back into my life.

You visited me briefly. Came and left unnoticed.

A glimmer of a shadow that paled in comparison to the identical impostor who was my permanent companion.

Then one day you came to reclaim your space.

With deliberate delicacy you unraveled my seamless tapestry.

Only to leave me alone and bewildered with a void so profound it shattered my soul.

You asked me to earn the privilege to play with you, to lay with you, to hold you in my arms once more.

I know not how, but I promise you this:

I am willing to try.

Life Goes On

Somewhere
Some place
Something
Someone

A child takes his first step
A young man is shot
An old building crumbles
And a fresh dream is born

Anguish and arousal
Ecstasy and trepidation
Separate events
Simultaneously experienced

A reunion of those long separated
And a separation of those long united
Occur in the same instant
A lifelong friendship is formed

When strangers interact
Emotions coalesce
And the core of humanity
Shines in shared understanding

The purpose of life
Debatable.
The beauty of life
It goes on.

Broken

What do you do...
When you come from a broken home
When you look for hope and see nothing
When you know there is no solution

Where do you go...
When the road ahead is dark
When the path behind you is lost
When the ground you stand on is giving way

How do you cope...
When your sadness comes from your blood
When the roots that nourish you stunt your own growth
When your destiny is a frightening shadow

Rhetorical questions
Borne of limitless pain
I ask not for the ease of a carefree mind

Only the strength to face tomorrow.

Darkness

What Is it like...

To know darkness
Unseen with the eyes
Felt in your mind

To suffocate from strangulation of the soul
Intangible and inescapable

To cry tears that fall not on your cheeks
But rather on your heart.

An oppressive force
Governing life with an iron grip

Penetrate this deceptive smile
A failing attempt at insubordination
Against the *darkness.*

Secret

A circle of friends forged only by circumstance
Unequivocally ephemeral.

An ordinary night; extraordinary circumstances
A latent truth revealed.

One woman's anguish; another's ultimate relief.
Every woman's nightmare.

An unforgettable tale devilishly delivered with humor
Though scented with shame

Innocent bystanders
Confidante casualties
Frozen in shock.

A bond we formed
Born of mutual understanding
Unmistakably permanent.

Foreigner

Pain and heartache
Deep and prolonged
For what?

Realization
Of expectations
Unfulfilled

Aspirations for the world
Expectations and hopes
Preparing for the worst
But secretly wishing...

Unfair
Unreal
Unacceptable.

Brothers of one blood
Sisters of the same heritage
With no shared love

Unrestrained selfishness
Selfless sacrifice
Pointless murder

The last of her kind
Wandering in unfriendly territories
Among the blind and heartless

A lost soul.

Orphan

A beauty born from pain
Nourished in toxicity
Watered with tears

Ever present
Flowers bloom in the desert
Of her heart.

A façade
Constructed of feigned relations
Herein lies her truth.

Until a blemish in the mirage
Reveals a palpable absence
Of real.

Shattered.

Tragedy

Brotherly love
Or blood-soaked hate?

The human connection
Or the deteriorating human condition?

A land of boundless dreams.
Or one of broken hopes?

An unrivaled world power.
We make leaps and bounds
Opening the gates to opportunity.

Yet we stumble and fall
In the most basic foundation to success
That of loving they neighbor.

We embrace individuality
And forget the individual.

A generation of aliens
A population without a soul.
30

Lost in the darkness.
We stand united.
And separate.

God help us.

Release

Three months, a single week and one final day.
One date turned into two; two turned into four.
And soon I found myself waking up next to you, hoping
you would never leave.

Time slowed down just enough for us to revel in the
honeymoon of first kisses and soft touches.
Passion vigilantly guarded our space, barring entry to
anything but careful breaches of comfort and exciting
waves of uncertainty.

The love I gave to you was real.

Unadulterated by the inevitable fact of change and
defiant to the subtle hints of a mismatch made in
Heaven.
The novelty of a love returned in equal force and twice
the sincerity was an intangible beauty that dwarfed any
shreds of clarity that may have remained in my mind.

I followed you. Blindly.

Because I had no choice.

Like a child whose curiosity and innocence cares not for cautionary comments, I rested my hand on the fiery stove top oblivious to the certainty of pain.

Like the delivery of an anesthetic, the sharp sting and burn gave way to a heavy sensation of numbness.
The space I created for you in my life transformed into a vacuum whose power defied resistance.
That new void that ached my heart was as palpable as the ice cold bed sheets that stayed empty where once your warmth resided.

Early on, I remembered only the blissful moments – sad times ironically having little significance to a hemorrhagic heart. The shine and sparkle of those perfect morsels of time, though ever real, have now faded to a dim glow.

As the sun sets on the memory of what used to be, the profound sadness endemic to our time together casts a shadow that still lingers. I struggle to reconcile the roller coaster of emotions and rationality that brewed a bittersweet cocktail cured to perfection in merely a 3 month time span.

Distance makes the heart grow fonder and yet time away
from the one you loved is nature's remedy for a broken
heart.

You may never understand the gravity of your words,
the authenticity of my intentions or the inscription you
left on my heart, but this you should know:

I am proud of the scar I hold because it is a permanent
reminder of the best mistake I ever made.

Lucky Number 26

Scientifically, our meeting will never make any sense. Years of trial and error, experimentation with countless subjects all yielding the Same. End. Result.

failure.

You entered my life on a whim. Call it stupidity, chance, rationalizing the irrational, hope, faith, or destiny, I deliberately chose to play the odds and gamble one final time. Our mutual understanding and agreement for a minimally pressured night out left me anything but carefree.

Everything was different – and wrong.
It was too soon. And far too late.
You were too far. I wasn't prepared to get so close.
It was a Sunday night. Who goes out on a Sunday night?
There was no parking. You were running late.

...And I was early.

I wasn't used to waiting. The unfounded pressure that
mounted as the minutes passed left me feeling foolish
and doubtful. Unconscious expectations slowly crept into
painful awareness and I was a deer in the headlights,
cognizant of only the fast approaching beams as you
walked through the door.

Maybe it was the sparkle in your eye
or the glint of your pink tie
perhaps the subtle bounce in your step,
or the slightly awkward pause that occurred after our
eyes met

that changed my world.

Headlights no longer blinded my vision as we conversed
comfortably in a dimly lit room. Expectations
disintegrated and happiness in its perfect form came to
reside in my heart.

It was the first of many firsts.
The first butterfly; the first laugh.
The first real electric attraction that took my breath
away.
The first compliment; my first blush.
The first time you kissed me; and that first intimate
touch.

Feeling vulnerable had never felt so right.

Now it is the crease in your forehead when you think,
your characteristic sigh that acknowledges the heaviness
of reality, and the purity of your soul in every word,
touch and look that we share that rocks my world into a
certainty I have never before experienced.

You are predictably unpredictable in a way that leaves
me comfortably uncomfortable.
You push me to grow, only to pull me even closer so we
can grow together.
Your raw honesty and simplicity is poignantly graceful
and something I treasure to my core.

I used to write poetry for you.
The you of the future.
The you that existed in my hidden dreams and deep
within my heart.

I wrote for a man who would enter my world and
breathe new life into my soul.

Today I see: your presence is my poetry, your touch is
my happiness and your eyes. Your kind eyes...

What can I say, I am one lucky girl.

Sheraan

They said he was a rare breed.
They worried she was a rare mistake.
What they had was a rare connection.

To the outside world, they were just two souls. Drifting.
But they traveled knowing their journey was already
charted.
Their destination was sewn into their blood and coursed
through their veins before they ever exchanged that first
look.

It was a meant-to-be story that they knew would arrive.
…if they were just willing to be patient.

So here we are. Eye to eye. Hand in hand.
Souls intertwined; standing at Fate's door.
Ready. Set. Home.